DADDY DO MY HAIR

Beth's Twists

*For Rahima. You are a beautiful
light in this world* — TO

*To my mum for always supporting
me with my dreams* — CT

The text in this book is an expanded version of the story
Daddy Do My Hair?: Beth's Twists by Tọlá Okogwu and Rahima Begum,
originally published by Florence Elizabeth Publishing in 2016.

SIMON & SCHUSTER

First published in Great Britain in 2022 by Simon & Schuster UK Ltd
1st Floor, 222 Gray's Inn Road, London WC1X 8HB

A CIP catalogue record for this book is available from
the British Library upon request

ISBN: 978-1-3985-1146-0 (PB)
ISBN: 978-1-3985-1147-7 (eBook)

Printed in China
1 3 5 7 9 10 8 6 4 2

FSC
www.fsc.org

MIX
Paper from
responsible sources
FSC® C144853

DADDY DO MY HAIR

Beth's Twists

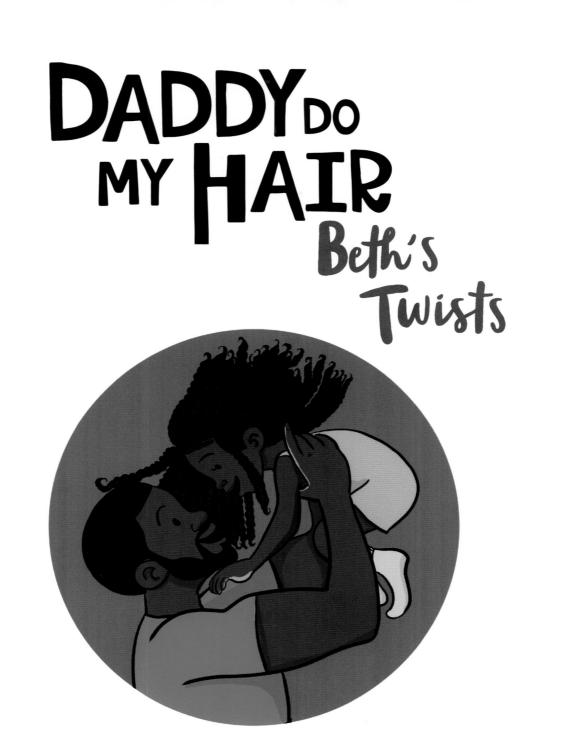

Tọlá Okogwu Chanté Timothy

SIMON & SCHUSTER

London New York Sydney Toronto New Delhi

It's Sunday evening and dinner is over.
Beth is excited and heads to the sofa . . .

Daddy is there with a smile and a chair.

"Daddy," she asks, "will you please do my hair?"

"Of course," says Daddy, and kisses her cheek,

For this is a question she asks every week.

This time that they spend is special and sweet,

Moments of fun
that feel like a treat.

"What style would you like
for School Picture Day?

Bunches like
last year,
with a bow on
display?"

"Or perhaps a braid-out, full and puffy?

Just like a cloud, all soft and fluffy."

"Can we do twists, please?
I'd like quite a few."

"A great idea, Beth!
They'll look pretty on you."

He starts by parting her hair like a pro.
His hands are so gentle,
they don't hurt her 'fro.

Daddy had to learn
to care for Beth's coils.

He didn't know to dampen,
then add the oils.

Daddy adds hair butter
to soften the strands.

Then crisscrosses the section
that rests in his hands.

He twists Beth's hair,
but not too tight.

They hang down her back
so bouncy and light.

Beth stares in the mirror at her big chunky twists,

Expertly done with a flick of Dad's wrists.

Just before bed,
so the twists stay in place,

Dad ties a bonnet
round Beth's smiling face.

That night, she dreams of that special time of theirs.

It makes her feel good to know that Dad cares.

The next day at school,
Beth walks in with pride.
Just look at her smiling
ever so wide.

She knows she looks great
from her head to her toes.

The picture will be epic
when she strikes a pose.

"Your twists look so special,"
says her friend Lee.

"We all look amazing,"
Beth answers with glee.

From Leon's waves to Tiwa's braids,

So many textures,
in so many shades.

Beth is ready, because picture time is here.

Her twists swing and sway from ear to ear.

"Which salon did them?"
her friends beg her to share.

"My Daddy's amazing.

He does my hair!"

About the Author

Tọlá Okogwu is a British-Nigerian Author, Journalist and Hair Care Educator. Born in Nigeria, but raised in London, she holds a Bachelor of Arts degree in Journalism. She has written for several publications, including Refinery29 and Black Ballad. Through her articles, online course, and coaching service, she has helped women all over the world improve the health of their hair.

Using her books and wider writing, Tọlá constantly seeks to create 'mirrors and windows', allowing children the opportunity to read books that are reflective of their own experiences, as well as other cultures. She is an avid reader who enjoys spending time with her family and friends in her home in Kent, where she lives with her husband and two daughters.

Hair Care Tips

I've learned a thing or two over the years about how to care for Afro-textured hair, so I thought I'd share a few of my top tips:

1. For Afro-textured hair to thrive, you need to keep it clean, moisturised and avoid handling and manipulating it too much.
2. Try not to over-wash Afro-textured hair as this can strip it of its natural oils and cause dryness and breakage. I recommend shampooing every 1-2 weeks.
3. Always detangle Afro-textured hair before shampooing it. When detangling, separate the hair into smaller sections, then dampen with water and apply an oil or a detangling product to provide slip. Starting from the ends, comb gently with a wide-tooth comb, working your way upwards. You can also detangle with your fingers first to minimise breakage.
4. Deep condition with a rich conditioner after every shampoo wash to replenish the hair and prevent dryness and breakage. Follow up with a leave-in conditioner before styling.
5. To prevent Afro-textured hair from becoming dry, moisturise it in between washes (every 2-5 days), starting with a hydrating spray, followed by a cream moisturiser and/or oil.
6. Use protective styles such as twists to reduce tangling and breakage. A silk bonnet, scarf or pillowcase can also help to protect hair from drying out at night and make protective styles last longer.

Recommended Products/Tools:

- Moisturising shampoo
- Moisturising deep conditioner
- Leave-in conditioner
- Light natural oil
- Hydrating spray
- Wide-tooth comb or detangling brush
- Silk scarf/bonnet